Tasty & Temp-ting

RECIPES

Making the most of your
Squoval™ Bakeware

•••••••••••••••••••••••••••••••••••••••

Tara McConnell Tesher

Author, Tara McConnell Tesher

Editors, Jodi Flayman, Merly Mesa, Carol Ginsburg

Recipe Development and Food Styling, Patty Rosenthal, Lynda Cannon

Photographers and Stylists, Freedom Martinez, Kelly Rusin

Post Production, Hal Silverman of Hal Silverman Studio

Cover and Page Design, Lorraine Dan of Grand Design

The paper in this printing meets the requirements of the ANSI Standard Z39.48-1992.

While every care has been taken in compiling the recipes for this book, the publisher, Cogin, Inc., or any other person who has been involved in working on this publication assumes no responsibility or liability for any errors or omissions, inadvertent or not, that may be found in the recipes or text, nor for any problems or damages that may arise as a result of preparing these recipes.

If food allergies or dietary restrictions are a concern, it is recommended that you carefully read ingredient product labels as well as consult a nutritionist or your physician to determine if a particular recipe meets your dietary needs.

We encourage you to use caution when working with all kitchen equipment and to always follow food safety guidelines.

To purchase this book for business or promotional use or to purchase more than 50 copies at a discount, or for custom editions, please contact Temp-tations LLC at the address below.

Inquiries should be addressed to:

Temp-tations LLC

180 Gordon Drive

Suite 103

Exton, PA 19341

ISBN: 978-0-9981635-7-4

Printed in the United States of America

First Edition

Table of Contents

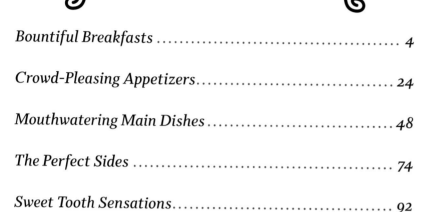

I'm so excited for you to use your Squoval™ bakeware!

This versatile set is going to become your new favorite in no time. In this book, you'll find more than 75 mouthwatering, quick & easy recipes (and some unexpected ways) to help you make the most of all the pieces. Enjoy!

Sara

Deep Dish Lid-It

Divided Lid-It

12-ounce Baker

4-quart Baker in rack

Plastic storage lids (not shown) are only meant to be used when storing at room temperature, in the refrigerator or freezer.

Bountiful Breakfasts

Eggs 'n' Ham Hash Breakfast

Serves 4

2 tablespoons vegetable oil

½ teaspoon garlic powder

½ teaspoon salt

¼ teaspoon black pepper, plus extra for sprinkling

2 (½-inch-thick) slices ham, cut into ½-inch cubes

3 cups refrigerated diced potatoes

½ cup diced onion

4 eggs

Sliced scallions for sprinkling

❖ Preheat oven to 425 degrees F. Coat a Squoval™ Deep Dish Lid-It with cooking spray.

❖ In a large bowl, combine oil, garlic powder, salt, and pepper; mix well. Add ham, potatoes, and onion; toss until evenly coated. Evenly spread mixture on Lid-It. Bake for 30 minutes or until potatoes begin to brown.

❖ Remove from oven and form 4 wells in the hash. (Check out the picture to see what I mean!) Gently crack an egg into each well. Bake for 5 to 7 more minutes or until egg whites are firm. Sprinkle with scallions and pepper, and serve immediately.

Tara Says: Yum! If you want, this easy breakfast can be started the night before. Just make your hash and keep it covered in the fridge. While the sleepyheads are getting up, all you need to do is pop it into the oven. Once it's warmed through, all that's left to do is add the eggs, bake 5 more minutes, and enjoy!

Strawberry Cheesecake French Toast Bake

Serves 8

1 (16-ounce) loaf French bread

1 (8-ounce) package cream cheese, softened

2 tablespoons powdered sugar

⅓ cup strawberry preserves

6 eggs

1-½ cups half-and-half

¼ cup plus 1 tablespoon granulated sugar, divided

1-½ cups coarsely crushed corn flakes

1 tablespoon butter, melted

¼ teaspoon ground cinnamon

❖ Coat a 4-quart Squoval™ Baker with cooking spray. Cut ends off bread and set aside or discard. Cut remaining bread into 16 slices, about 1 inch thick. Place half of the bread into baker, cut-side up, in one even layer.

❖ In a medium bowl, combine cream cheese and powdered sugar; mix well, then stir in preserves. Spread mixture evenly over each slice of bread in baker, then top with remaining slices of bread.

❖ In a large bowl, whisk eggs, half-and-half, and ¼ cup granulated sugar until well combined. Pour mixture evenly over bread. Cover and refrigerate for 1 hour or overnight, until liquid is almost absorbed.

❖ Preheat oven to 400 degrees F. In a bowl, combine crushed corn flakes, butter, remaining 1 tablespoon granulated sugar, and cinnamon; mix well. Sprinkle evenly over bread. Bake for 35 to 40 minutes or until set in center and golden brown. (Check out a photo of this on page 5.)

Tara Says: I love a good dessert-for-breakfast kind of morning. It practically ensures that you're going to have a "sweet" day! With this recipe, everyone gets their own French toast "sandwich" bake. And there's no need to bring out the syrup, since there's plenty of creamy fruit filling in every forkful. (Yes, this is the kind of "sandwich" you eat with a fork -- otherwise, things might get messy!)

All-In-One Breakfast for Two

Serves 2

1-½ cups frozen diced potatoes

¼ teaspoon salt

¼ teaspoon black pepper

4 eggs

¼ cup shredded cheddar cheese

Bacon bits for garnish (optional)

❊ Coat 2 (12-ounce) Squoval™ Bakers with cooking spray.

❊ In a small bowl, combine potatoes, salt, and pepper; mix well. Divide potato mixture evenly between the bakers. Microwave for 4 to 5 minutes or until hot.

❊ Meanwhile, in the same small bowl, beat eggs; add cheese and mix well. Divide egg mixture evenly between bakers, stir gently, and microwave for 1 minute; stir again, and continue cooking for 1-½ more minutes or until egg is set.

❊ Top with bacon bits, if desired. (In my kitchen, this isn't an option, it's a must-have.)

Tara Says: On busy mornings, it's hard to make a full breakfast for two. But I'm not the kind of gal who likes to skip out on breakfast, so I came up with this easy recipe that uses only one bowl and a couple of small bakers. (That's a clean-up win!) Plus this is an easy one to make your own. For starters, you can switch up the cheese -- try a Swiss or Mexican blend next time.

The Ultimate Italian Frittata

Serves 4 to 6

8 extra-large eggs

¼ cup milk

1 teaspoon Italian seasoning

1 teaspoon garlic powder

½ teaspoon salt

½ pound deli salami, diced

1-½ cups shredded
mozzarella cheese

½ cup chopped roasted
red peppers

½ cup sliced black olives

3-½ cups frozen diced
potatoes, thawed

2 tablespoons chopped
fresh basil

❖ Preheat oven to 400 degrees F. Coat a 4-quart Squoval™ Baker with cooking spray.

❖ In a medium bowl, whisk eggs, milk, Italian seasoning, garlic powder, and salt until well combined. Add remaining ingredients; mix well.

❖ Pour into baker and bake for 35 to 40 minutes or until firm in center. Allow to sit for 5 minutes, then cut and serve.

Tara Says: How about having an antipasto for breakfast? You got it! (You should know by now that I love coming up with new ways to eat old favorites.) This one is loaded with some of my favorite antipasto ingredients. Sometimes I'll even put out a bowl of grated Parmesan cheese, so that everyone can sprinkle on a little extra.

Bed & Breakfast Buttermilk Pancakes

Serves 3 to 4

2 cups all-purpose flour

⅓ cup sugar

2 teaspoons baking powder

½ teaspoon baking soda

½ teaspoon salt

2 eggs

2 cups buttermilk

2 tablespoons butter, melted, plus extra for cooking

❖ In a large bowl, combine flour, sugar, baking powder, baking soda, and salt; mix well. In a medium bowl, beat eggs, buttermilk, and 2 tablespoons melted butter; stir into dry ingredients until just combined. (Be careful not to overmix the batter or you'll end up with lots of air bubbles in your pancakes.)

❖ Preheat oven to 200 degrees F. On a griddle pan or in a large skillet over medium heat, melt 1 tablespoon butter. Pour about ⅓ cup of batter onto griddle. Cook for 2 to 3 minutes or until bubbles begin to form, then with a spatula, turn over and cook for 2 more minutes or until golden brown.

❖ Place cooked pancakes in a 4-quart Squoval™ Baker and cover with aluminum foil; place in the oven to keep warm while you make the rest of the pancakes. Repeat with remaining batter, adding more butter to the griddle as needed. (Check out the photo on page 4.)

Tara Says: Here's how I like my pancakes: hot and dripping with melted butter. Here's how I don't like my pancakes: cold and rubbery. So when I realized that I could keep pancakes warm by placing them inside of a 4-quart Squoval Baker, covered with foil in a warm oven, I was thrilled. Oh, and if any kids are reading this, this is a great way to treat mom and dad with breakfast in bed. Trust me, they're going to love this.

The Butcher's Breakfast Sausage

Makes 10 patties

1 pound ground pork

2 teaspoons ground sage

¾ teaspoon salt

¾ teaspoon black pepper

⅛ teaspoon ground nutmeg

✺ Preheat oven to 425 degrees F. Coat a Squoval™ Deep Dish Lid-It with cooking spray.

✺ In a medium bowl, combine all ingredients; mix well. Form mixture into 10 equal patties and place on Lid-It.

✺ Bake for 10 minutes; turn over and continue to cook for 8 to 10 more minutes or until no longer pink in center. (Check out the photo on page 4.)

Tara Says: As a self-described sausage connoisseur, I've sampled my fair share of sausage varieties. While there are plenty of prepackaged links and patties that taste great, I have to admit, every once in a while it's fun to play the role of "butcher" and make my own. These are great served alongside scrambled eggs or a big stack of my buttermilk pancakes (page 12). And sure, you can make these ahead of time, but I think they taste best when they're served right out of the oven.

Very Berry Dutch Pancake

Serves 6 to 8

½ stick butter, melted

6 eggs

1 cup milk

½ teaspoon salt

1 cup all-purpose flour

2 cups sliced strawberries

1 cup blackberries

1 cup raspberries

¾ cup blueberries

Powdered sugar
for sprinkling

❀ Preheat oven to 425 degrees F. Pour melted butter into a 4-quart Squoval™ Baker; set aside.

❀ In a blender, combine eggs, milk, and salt; blend until frothy. (This is what makes the pancake puff up.) Add flour and blend again until well mixed. Pour egg mixture into baker.

❀ Bake for 25 to 30 minutes or until edges puff up, the center is set, and the whole thing is golden.

❀ Carefully remove from oven and top with strawberries, blackberries, raspberries, and blueberries. Sprinkle with powdered sugar and serve immediately.

Tara Says: I love the classic combination of pancakes, berries, and whipped cream. Top this off with your favorite, whether that's homemade, from a can, or out of a container. And if you like whipped cream half as much as I do, be generous with your dollops! It makes this breakfast treat even better.

Peanut Butter Banana Overnight Oats

Serves 1

1 small ripe banana

½ cup old-fashioned oats

⅓ cup milk

2 tablespoons vanilla yogurt

1 tablespoon peanut butter

2 teaspoons honey

½ teaspoon
ground cinnamon

❁ In a 12-ounce Squoval™ Baker, mash banana with a fork. Add remaining ingredients, mix well, and cover with a plastic lid.

❁ Refrigerate overnight. Stir before serving.

Tara Says: Here's another one for those grab-and-go kind of mornings. If you've never heard of overnight oats before, it's simply oatmeal that steeps in the fridge overnight. There are hundreds of ways to make it, using fruit, nuts, and other toppings -- this is one of my favorites. It's packed with protein, thanks to the yogurt and peanut butter, and features the goodness of honey and banana. It's a satisfying, sweet, and energizing way to start your day.

Broccoli & Cheese Breakfast Casserole

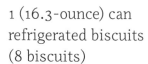

Serves 8 to 12

1 (16.3-ounce) can refrigerated biscuits (8 biscuits)

1 (10.2-ounce) can refrigerated biscuits (5 biscuits)

12 eggs

⅓ cup milk

½ teaspoon salt

¼ teaspoon black pepper

1-½ cups diced ham

1 (12-ounce) package frozen broccoli florets, thawed, coarsely chopped

2-¼ cups shredded cheddar cheese, divided

❖ Preheat oven to 375 degrees F. Coat a 4-quart Squoval™ Baker with cooking spray.

❖ Cut each biscuit into 6 pieces.

❖ In a large bowl, whisk together eggs, milk, salt, and pepper until well mixed. Stir in ham, broccoli, and 2 cups cheese. Add biscuit pieces and toss to coat evenly. Pour mixture into baker.

❖ Bake for 45 minutes, cover with aluminum foil; continue cooking for 10 more minutes or until center is set. Sprinkle remaining cheese on top and return to oven, uncovered, just until cheese is melted. (Check out the photo on page 5.)

Tara Says: If you're wondering why I don't use already chopped frozen broccoli, it's because I like having the bigger pieces in my bake. (You get more pops of color!) Since almost everyone I know eats with their eyes first … it just made sense to me! Of course, if all you have on hand is the chopped kind, you can certainly make the swap.

Really Good Granola Brittle

Serves 10 to 12

2 cups rolled oats

1 cup slivered almonds

1 cup dried cranberries

¾ cup chopped pecans

½ cup roasted sunflower seeds

¼ cup sesame seeds

½ cup honey

⅓ cup canola oil

2 teaspoons vanilla extract

⅔ cup light brown sugar

❈ Preheat oven to 350 degrees F. Line a Squoval™ Deep Dish Lid-It with foil and coat lightly with cooking spray.

❈ In a large bowl, combine oats, almonds, cranberries, pecans, sunflower seeds, and sesame seeds.

❈ In a saucepan over low heat, combine honey, oil, vanilla, and brown sugar, and bring to a boil. (Once it starts to boil, take it right off the heat. Be careful not to overcook or you'll end up with rock-hard granola.) Remove from heat and pour over nut mixture; stir until evenly coated. Spread mixture evenly on Lid-It.

❈ Bake for 35 to 40 minutes or until browned. After it cools slightly (it should still be a little warm), break apart into pieces and allow to cool completely. Store in an airtight container. (See photo on page 5.)

Tara Says: I hardly buy premade granola anymore. It's so easy to make your own and load it up with the things you love most. I like to put the smaller pieces on yogurt, ice cream, and in salads. The larger pieces make a perfect grab-and-go snack, especially when you need a little pick-me-up in the middle of the day. Just keep a little baggie in your car or in your purse at all times and you'll be good to go!

Anytime Cinnamon Buns

Makes 8 buns

¾ cup light brown sugar

1 tablespoon ground cinnamon

1 pound frozen bread dough, thawed

½ stick butter, melted

⅓ cup chopped walnuts

Cream Cheese Icing

4 ounces cream cheese, softened

1 tablespoon butter, softened

1-½ cups powdered sugar

❀ Coat a Squoval™ Deep Dish Lid-It with cooking spray.

❀ In a small bowl, combine brown sugar and cinnamon; set aside.

❀ On a lightly floured surface, roll dough into a 12- x 14-inch rectangle. (Make sure you dust your rolling pin with a bit of flour, so it doesn't stick.) Brush dough with butter and sprinkle evenly with sugar mixture and nuts.

❀ Starting with the short end, roll the dough up jelly-roll style and place seam-side down. Cut into 8 slices and place cut-side up on Lid-It. Cover with plastic wrap and let rise for 1-½ to 2 hours or until doubled in size.

❀ Preheat oven to 375 degrees F. Bake rolls for 18 to 20 minutes or until golden brown.

❀ Meanwhile to make Cream Cheese Icing, in a medium bowl with an electric mixer, beat cream cheese, butter, and powdered sugar until smooth. Spread icing over each bun and serve warm.

Tara Says: Cinnamon buns and all things related are kind of a big deal in my house. We love our cinnamon! So it's not unusual for us to make these all year round. In the fall, I'll sometimes add a little maple syrup to the icing to make these even cozier. Come summertime, a few drops of lemon extract adds the perfect dose of sunshine to these beauties.

Blueberry Patch Oatmeal Bars

Makes 21 bars

2 cups old-fashioned oats

2 cups all-purpose flour

1-¼ cups brown sugar

¾ cup chopped walnuts

1-½ teaspoons baking soda

½ teaspoon salt

2 sticks butter, melted

3 cups fresh or frozen and thawed blueberries

¼ cup granulated sugar

1 teaspoon cornstarch

❀ Preheat oven to 350 degrees F. In a large bowl, combine oats, flour, brown sugar, walnuts, baking soda, and salt; pour butter over mixture and mix until crumbly. Press half of the oat mixture into a Squoval™ Deep Dish Lid-It.

❀ In a separate bowl, combine blueberries, granulated sugar, and cornstarch. Mix until blueberries are evenly coated, then sprinkle blueberries evenly over oat mixture in Lid-It. Sprinkle with remaining oat mixture.

❀ Bake for 30 to 35 minutes or until golden brown. Let cool completely before cutting.

Tara Says: Satisfy your morning sweet tooth with this sweet blueberry treat. It goes great with a cup of coffee or (if you're not a coffee drinker) a glass of cold milk. Don't worry about having too many of these on hand -- they freeze really well! Just cut them into bars, wrap them up, and pop them in the freezer. And when you're ready for one, simply take it out and it'll thaw in minutes.

Crowd-Pleasing Appetizers

Honey-Kissed Goat Cheese Balls

Makes 24 balls

¾ cup Italian-style Panko bread crumbs

¼ cup walnuts, finely chopped

2 eggs

1 tablespoon water

2 goat cheese logs, 8 ounces each

Cooking spray

Honey for drizzling

❀ Preheat oven to 450 degrees F. Coat a Squoval™ Deep Dish Lid-It with cooking spray.

❀ In a shallow dish, combine bread crumbs and walnuts; mix well. In another shallow dish, whisk eggs and water; set aside.

❀ Cut each cheese log into 12 slices and using your hands, roll each slice into a ball (about the size of a walnut). Dip each cheese ball into egg mixture, then roll in bread crumb mixture until evenly coated on all sides. Place on Lid-It and lightly spray with cooking spray.

❀ Bake for 7 to 8 minutes or until golden. Cool slightly, then drizzle with honey and serve.

Tara Says: Honey and goat cheese are a match made in taste bud heaven. They just complement each other so perfectly! I love how gourmet these look and taste with minimal effort. And if you garnish them with a few sprigs of fresh rosemary (like I did in the photo), they get even better. Serve these the next time you've got company, and prepare for plenty of "Mmms!"

Chicken Strips with Raspberry-Chili Sauce

Serves 4 to 5

4 cups corn flakes, crushed

½ teaspoon garlic powder

½ teaspoon onion powder

½ teaspoon salt

¼ teaspoon black pepper

2 eggs

¼ cup milk

1-½ pounds boneless, skinless chicken breasts, cut into 2-inch strips

Cooking spray

Raspberry-Chili Sauce

½ cup seedless raspberry jam

¼ cup sweet Thai chili sauce

Preheat oven to 375 degrees F. Coat a Squoval™ Deep Dish Lid-It with cooking spray.

In a large plastic storage bag, combine corn flakes, garlic powder, onion powder, salt, and pepper; mix well and set aside. In a large bowl, whisk eggs and milk. Add chicken strips to egg mixture and let sit for about 15 minutes. Remove chicken strips, one at a time, from egg mixture and toss in corn flake mixture, shaking well to coat. Place on Lid-It and repeat until all the chicken is breaded.

Lightly spray with cooking spray. Bake for 15 minutes or until golden brown and no longer pink in center.

Meanwhile to make the Raspberry-Chili Sauce, in a 12-ounce Squoval™ Baker, whisk raspberry jam and chili sauce until smooth. To serve, drizzle chicken strips with sauce mixture and enjoy.

Tara Says: Chicken strips are good on their own, but they're even better with an extra-crispy coating. These strips are tender on the inside, crunchy on the outside, and drizzled with the easiest (and tastiest!) sauce you'll ever make. Not only does it add the perfect amount of sweetness, but the sauce gives it a little zip that's just heavenly. And bonus! -- it adds some color to your appetizer spread.

Holiday Baked Maple-Pecan Brie

Serves 6 to 8

1 (8-ounce) round brie cheese

1 teaspoon brown sugar

2 tablespoons butter

½ cup coarsely chopped pecans

¼ cup maple syrup

½ teaspoon orange zest

¼ teaspoon ground cinnamon

¼ cup dried cherries

Veggies and crackers for serving

❖ Preheat oven to 350 degrees F. Coat the center of a Squoval™ Divided Lid-It with cooking spray.

❖ Place cheese in center of Lid-It; sprinkle brown sugar on top and press down lightly. Bake for 10 to 12 minutes or until cheese begins to soften.

❖ Meanwhile, in a small skillet over low heat, melt butter. Add pecans and toast for 3 minutes. (Keep an eye on these, so they don't burn.) Add syrup, orange zest, cinnamon, and dried cherries; heat for 2 minutes. Spoon pecan mixture over cheese and place veggies and crackers in outer sections of Lid-It for serving.

Tara Says: This is the perfect dish to whip up when unexpected company drops in. The ingredients are basic enough that you could always have them on hand. That means as soon as the doorbell rings, you can have this ready to serve in about 20 minutes. And with the holiday-special glaze, it doesn't get much better than this.

Simply Delish Homemade Hummus

Serves 6 to 8

2 (15-ounce) cans garbanzo beans, drained, with ⅓ cup liquid reserved

2 garlic cloves

3 tablespoons olive oil

2 tablespoons fresh lemon juice

1 teaspoon sea salt

1 teaspoon ground cumin

¼ teaspoon coarsely ground black pepper

* In a food processor, combine all ingredients, including reserved liquid. Process until mixture is smooth and no lumps remain, scraping down the sides of the container as needed.

* Serve immediately or cover and chill until ready to serve.

5-Minute Red Pepper Hummus

Serves 6 to 8

2 (15-ounce) cans garbanzo beans, drained, with ⅓ cup liquid reserved

1 (12-ounce) jar roasted red peppers, drained

3 garlic cloves

2 tablespoons fresh lemon juice

2 tablespoons olive oil

1 teaspoon ground cumin

1 teaspoon salt

* See instructions above.

 Tara Says: When I entertain, I like giving my friends and family lots of options, so when I know I've got company coming over, I make both of these recipes. Then, I serve them in two of the sections of the Squoval Divided Lid-It. The other section gets filled with sliced pita bread, crackers, or crisp cut-up veggies. Easy peasy....!

Buffalo Wing Bread Bowl Dip

Serves 8 to 10

1 (1-pound) oval loaf rye or Italian bread, unsliced

1 (8-ounce) package cream cheese, softened

2 cups shredded mozzarella cheese

¾ cup chopped celery

½ cup blue cheese crumbles

¼ cup buffalo wing sauce

1-½ cups shredded cooked chicken breast

❖ Preheat oven to 375 degrees F. Cut the top off of the bread (about ⅓ of the way down) and set top aside. Create a bread bowl by hollowing out the inside, leaving about 1 inch of bread around edges. (See photo.) Cut top of the bread and the bread that you removed into cubes; set aside.

❖ In a large bowl, mix together remaining ingredients until thoroughly combined. Spoon mixture into bread loaf, then loosely wrap bread in aluminum foil. Place on a Squoval™ Deep Dish Lid-It.

❖ Bake for 40 to 45 minutes or until hot in center. Carefully remove foil and serve on Lid-It surrounded by bread cubes and fresh-cut veggies.

 Tara Says: If you can't find an unsliced oval bread in your grocery store, you can always ask a baker in the bakery department if they could make one for you the next day. Most of the time, grocery stores are more than happy to do this. Plus, there's nothing like freshly baked bread! PS. This dip is a crowd favorite, especially when it's served on game days.

Parmesan-Crusted Dilly Crab Crocks

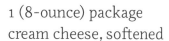

Serves 8 to 10

1 (8-ounce) package cream cheese, softened

½ pound imitation crabmeat, flaked

2 teaspoons lemon juice

2 teaspoons fresh chopped dill

½ teaspoon garlic powder

2 tablespoons grated Parmesan cheese, plus extra for sprinkling

❖ Preheat oven to 350 degrees F.

❖ In a medium bowl, combine all ingredients; mix well. Spoon mixture into 2 (12-ounce) Squoval™ Bakers.

❖ Sprinkle lightly with extra Parmesan cheese. Bake for 30 to 35 minutes or until hot in center; serve immediately.

Tara Says: This dip is creamy, dreamy, and totally deserving to be on the table the next time you've got company coming over. Serve it with your favorite crackers or some crispy breadsticks and set out a few wedges of lemon, so that everyone can squeeze on a little extra sunshine. (Aren't the cute little bakers perfect for this?!)

The Very Best Shrimp Cocktail

Serves 4

8 cups (2 quarts) water

4 sprigs fresh thyme

1 rib celery, chopped

1 small onion, chopped

3 tablespoons fresh lemon juice, divided

1-½ pounds large or colossal raw shrimp, peeled and deveined, with tails left on

1 cup ketchup

2 tablespoons tomato paste

3 tablespoons prepared white horseradish, drained

In a soup pot over high heat, bring water, thyme, celery, onion, and 2 tablespoons lemon juice to a boil. Add the shrimp and cook for 2 to 3 minutes or until shrimp are pink and cooked through. Drain and chill for at least 2 hours.

Meanwhile, in a medium bowl, combine ketchup, tomato paste, horseradish, and the remaining 1 tablespoon lemon juice; mix well.

Cover and chill until ready to serve. Fill a 4-quart Squoval™ Baker with ice. Place shrimp on a Squoval Deep Dish Lid-It and set on top of ice (This will keep your shrimp nice and chilled). Place cocktail sauce in a 12-ounce Squoval Baker and serve.

Tara Says: There are three important pieces to making the best shrimp cocktail. First, you need to start with big, plump shrimp (that's why I like the colossal kind!). Second, you've got to have a perfect sweet and zingy cocktail sauce (and homemade is always better than store-bought). Finally, you have to present it in style! I bet you never thought of using your 4-quart Baker to keep the Lid-It chilled, but once you put this together, it's hard not to be impressed.

French Bistro Stuffed Mushrooms

Makes 12 mushrooms

1 pound large white mushrooms

3 tablespoons butter

½ cup finely chopped onion

1 packet onion soup mix

1 tablespoon water

¼ cup plain bread crumbs

⅛ teaspoon black pepper

3 slices Swiss cheese, each slice cut into 4 squares

❀ Preheat oven to 375 degrees F. Gently clean mushrooms by wiping them with damp paper towels. (Don't wash the mushrooms under running water or they'll become mushy.) Remove stems from 12 mushrooms; set aside caps. Finely chop mushroom stems and remaining whole mushrooms.

❀ In a large skillet over medium heat, melt butter; cook onion for 3 minutes or just until soft. Stir in chopped mushrooms, onion soup mix, and water and cook for 4 to 5 minutes or until tender. Remove from heat and add bread crumbs and black pepper; mix well.

❀ Using a small spoon, fill mushroom caps with stuffing mixture. Place on a Squoval™ Deep Dish Lid-It.

❀ Bake for 12 minutes. Remove from oven, top each with a piece of cheese, and return to oven for 5 minutes or until cheese is melted and mushrooms are heated through. Serve immediately.

Tara Says: This is one of those great recipes you can make and take to any get-together. They can be assembled in advance and kept in the fridge for a day or two before baking. (Just find out if you can use the oven at whoever's house you're going to!) The best thing about these stuffed mushrooms is that they taste just like a bowl of onion soup you'd find at a French bistro.

Easy Ranch Cheeseball Snowman

Serves 10 to 12

2 (8-ounce) packages
cream cheese, softened

1 (3-ounce) package
real bacon bits

1 cup finely chopped walnuts

¼ cup ranch salad dressing

2 scallions, finely chopped

¼ cup chopped fresh parsley

Peppercorns and crackers
for decorating

❖ In a large bowl, combine all ingredients except peppercorns and crackers; mix well.

❖ Divide mixture into three balls: one small, one medium, and one large. Arrange balls on a Squoval™ Deep Dish Lid-It to form a snowman. (See photo.)

❖ Decorate cheese balls with peppercorns and crackers, like I did, or use your creativity and have some fun. Cover and chill until ready to serve.

Tara Says: Not only does this guy work as a centerpiece for your appetizer spread, but everyone can dig in too! I just love how easy this is to make. In fact, I suggest letting the kids help, for some extra family fun. Once he's all dolled up and ready to go, surround him with a colorful assortment of your favorite veggies and crackers for lots of dipping and spreading.

Hot & Hearty Nachos Supreme

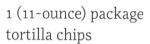

Serves 8 to 10

1 (11-ounce) package tortilla chips

1 (16-ounce) can refried beans

1 (1-¼-ounce) packet taco seasoning mix

2 cups (8 ounces) shredded Colby-Jack cheese

1 cup guacamole

2 scallions, thinly sliced

1 large tomato, chopped

1 jalapeño pepper, thinly sliced (optional)

❀ Preheat oven to 350 degrees F. Place tortilla chips in a 4-quart Squoval™ Baker. In a medium microwave-safe bowl, stir refried beans and taco seasoning mix. Microwave for 1 to 2 minutes or until warm; spoon over tortilla chips.

❀ Sprinkle cheese over bean mixture and bake for 3 to 5 minutes or until cheese is melted. Dollop with guacamole, then sprinkle with scallions, tomato, and jalapeño slices, if desired. Serve immediately.

Tara Says: If you're a regular QVC fan or own any of my cookbooks, then you already know how I feel about anything Tex-Mex -- I love it. So naturally, nachos are a favorite. You can take these up a notch by adding some cooked shredded chicken or beef and dollops of sour cream. And the nice thing about serving your nachos in a deep baking dish like this is, you don't have to worry about your beans getting cold, since the ceramic retains the heat.

Pizzeria-Style Italian Stromboli

Serves 6 to 8

1 (13.8-ounce) can refrigerated pizza crust

8 slices Genoa or hard salami

8 slices mozzarella cheese

6 slices deli-style ham

½ cup roasted red peppers, drained, and cut into strips

1 tablespoon Parmesan cheese

½ teaspoon garlic powder

⅛ teaspoon salt

⅛ teaspoon black pepper

Cooking spray

1 teaspoon Italian seasoning

❀ Preheat oven to 425°F. Coat a Squoval™ Deep Dish Lid-It with cooking spray.

❀ Unroll pizza dough onto a flat surface. Layer with salami, mozzarella cheese, ham, and roasted red pepper strips. Sprinkle with Parmesan cheese, garlic powder, salt, and black pepper.

❀ Starting with the long end of the dough, roll up jellyroll-style and place on Lid-It. Lightly spray stromboli with cooking spray, then sprinkle with Italian seasoning.

❀ Bake for 15 to 18 minutes or until golden. Let cool for 5 minutes, then slice and serve.

Tara Says: Your favorite Italian ingredients all rolled up into one -- how could you go wrong? This app is going to be popular with everyone in your house, from the kids to mom and dad. I like to set this out with a small baker full of spaghetti sauce, so that everyone can dunk away.

Jumbo Lump Crab Cake Bites

Makes 2 dozen bites

1 egg

1 tablespoon mayonnaise

1 teaspoon seafood seasoning (like Old Bay)

1 teaspoon Dijon mustard

8 saltine crackers, finely crushed

1 pound jumbo lump crabmeat

❀ Preheat oven to 350°F. Coat a Squoval™ Deep Dish Lid-It with cooking spray.

❀ In a large bowl, lightly beat egg. Add mayonnaise, seafood seasoning, mustard, and crushed crackers; mix well.

❀ Gently stir in crabmeat, until thoroughly combined. Shape mixture by tablespoonfuls into 24 patties and place on Lid-It.

❀ Bake for 12 to 15 minutes or until lightly browned.

Tara Says: You know I love to dip things, so when I make these crab cakes, I whip up a tangy mustard sauce to go with them. To make it, I start by whisking together 1 cup of mayonnaise with 1 tablespoon plus 1/2 teaspoon of dry mustard in a 12-ounce Squoval Baker. Then I whisk in 2 tablespoons of heavy cream, 2 tablespoons of milk, 2 teaspoons of Worcestershire sauce, 1 teaspoon of steak sauce, and a little salt. I chill it for a bit and it's ready for dipping!

Great Greek Flatbread

Serves 4 to 5

1 (11-ounce) can refrigerated thin pizza crust

⅓ cup refrigerated garlic and herb cheese spread

¼ cup pitted Kalamata olives, sliced in half lengthwise

¼ cup chopped roasted red peppers, drained, and patted dry

¼ cup crumbled feta cheese

Dried oregano for sprinkling

❖ Preheat oven to 400 degrees F. Coat a Squoval™ Deep Dish Lid-It with cooking spray.

❖ Unroll pizza crust onto Lid-It. Using your fingers, press dough against the sides and roll edges under, creating a border. (See photo.) Using a fork, prick dough. Bake for 8 minutes or until dough begins to brown.

❖ Remove crust from oven and spread with herb cheese. Top evenly with olives, roasted red peppers, and feta cheese. Sprinkle with oregano. Bake for 6 to 8 minutes or until crust is golden brown. Cut into pieces and serve.

Tara Says: If you love Greek salad, then there's a good chance you're going to love this easy appetizer inspired by some of the best flavors in the Mediterranean. This is a fresh and healthy option to offer your family and guests. You can even customize it with more goodness, like adding artichokes or with a different variety of olives. (Have you ever checked out the olive bar at your local gourmet grocery store -- there are so many choices!)

Hula Hula Cocktail Meatballs

Serves 12 to 15

1 (12-ounce) jar sweet and sour sauce

¼ cup soy sauce

¼ cup light brown sugar

½ teaspoon ground ginger

1 (32-ounce) package bite-sized frozen meatballs

1 cup frozen mango chunks

1 cup frozen pineapple chunks

❀ Preheat oven to 375 degrees F.

❀ In a 4-quart Squoval™ Baker, combine sweet and sour sauce, soy sauce, brown sugar, and ginger; mix well. Stir in meatballs, mango, and pineapple chunks. Cover with a Squoval Deep Dish Lid-It and bake for 35 to 40 minutes or until meatballs are heated through. (See photo on page 25.)

 Tara Says: These meatballs are so awesome, they make other meatballs jealous. Not only do they make the perfect appetizer for almost any occasion, but when you're looking for a change-of-pace main dish, try serving these over some cooked basmati rice (to soak up the sauce!). No matter how you serve them, everyone's going to love their tropical flavor.

Spinach Artichoke Party Toasts

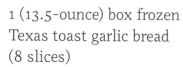

Serves 8 to 10

1 (13.5-ounce) box frozen Texas toast garlic bread (8 slices)

1 (9-ounce) package frozen creamed spinach

1 (14-ounce) can artichokes, drained and chopped

3 tablespoons grated Parmesan cheese, divided

½ teaspoon onion powder

1 cup shredded mozzarella cheese

❊ Preheat oven to 400 degrees F. Place garlic bread on a Squoval™ Deep Dish Lid-It and bake for 8 to 9 minutes or until lightly toasted.

❊ Meanwhile, heat spinach according to package directions and place in a medium bowl. Stir in artichokes, 2 tablespoons Parmesan cheese, and the onion powder. Evenly spoon mixture onto slices of bread. Sprinkle with mozzarella cheese and remaining Parmesan cheese.

❊ Bake for 8 to 10 minutes or until hot in center and cheese is melted. Cut each slice diagonally in quarters and serve piping hot.

Tara Says: Some of the best things in life are covered in cheese...and that includes thick-cut, garlicky Texas toast. (I'm practically swooning just thinking about it right now!) This appetizer delivers BIG flavor and creaminess. Actually, every time I've made it, it's disappeared before I could get another helping, so you might want to make a double batch!

Marvelous Main Dishes

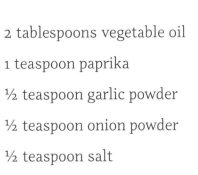

Lemon-Rosemary Roasted Chicken

Serves 4 to 5

2 tablespoons vegetable oil

1 teaspoon paprika

½ teaspoon garlic powder

½ teaspoon onion powder

½ teaspoon salt

½ teaspoon black pepper

1 (4- to 4-½-pound) chicken

4 sprigs fresh rosemary, plus extra for garnish

2 lemons, cut in half, divided

❖ Preheat oven to 350 degrees F. In a small bowl, combine oil, paprika, garlic powder, onion powder, salt, and pepper.

❖ Place chicken in a 4-quart Squoval™ Baker and rub with seasoning mixture until completely coated. Stuff the 4 rosemary sprigs and 2 lemon halves inside chicken's cavity. Squeeze remaining lemon halves over chicken, then place in baker.

❖ Bake uncovered for 1-¼ to 1-½ hours or until juices run clear, basting occasionally with pan juices. Remove from oven, discard rosemary and lemon, and let chicken rest for 5 minutes before cutting. Garnish with fresh rosemary and serve.

 Tara Says: One of the things I love about the 4-quart Squoval Baker is that it's so versatile. Not only can you roast a whole chicken in it, but it's also perfect for baking, mixing, storing, and serving. And it does it all in style! (By the way, for an even fancier presentation, you can serve this on the Squoval Deep Dish Lid-It!)

Crave-Worthy California Cobb

Serves 6 to 8

2 boneless, skinless chicken breasts, lightly pounded

Salt and pepper for seasoning

1 head iceberg lettuce, cut into bite-sized pieces

½ head romaine lettuce, cut into bite-sized pieces

8 slices crispy cooked bacon, crumbled

3 hard-boiled eggs, cut into wedges

2 avocados, peeled, pitted, and cut into ½-inch slices

1 cup cherry tomatoes, cut in half

¼ pound blue cheese, crumbled

1 cup ranch dressing

❖ Season chicken with salt and pepper. Coat a large skillet with cooking spray; over medium-high heat cook chicken 4 to 5 minutes per side or until golden and no pink remains. Remove chicken, set aside to cool slightly, then cut into ½-inch chunks.

❖ Meanwhile, mix both types of lettuce in a 4-quart Squoval™ Baker. Arrange cooked chicken, bacon, eggs, avocado, tomato, and blue cheese, in rows, on top of lettuce. (See photo.)

❖ When ready to serve, drizzle with ranch dressing.

 Tara Says: I know everyone isn't crazy about main dish salads, but this one is usually the exception. Maybe it's because there's a lot going on -- you've got eggs, chicken, cheese, avocado...oh, and bacon. (Who can resist?!) I love arranging the toppings in rows because it gives the salad a "buffet" feel. And in case you were wondering, the large Squoval Baker is perfect for this because it holds in the cold, so everything stays fresh and chilled!

Creamy Chicken & Broccoli Bake

Serves 4 to 6

1-½ cups coarsely crushed butter-flavored crackers

½ stick butter, melted

2 cups cooked chicken breast chunks

1 (8-ounce) can water chestnuts, drained and chopped

1 (16-ounce) package frozen broccoli florets

1 (10-½-ounce) can condensed cream of chicken soup

1 (10-½-ounce) can condensed cream of mushroom soup

1 cup sour cream

½ cup water

1 clove garlic, minced

1 teaspoon dried basil

¼ teaspoon black pepper

❖ Preheat oven to 325 degrees F. Coat a 4-quart Squoval™ Baker with cooking spray. In a small bowl, combine crushed crackers and butter; mix well.

❖ Evenly distribute chicken in baker. Sprinkle water chestnuts and broccoli over chicken.

❖ In a large bowl, combine chicken and mushroom soups, sour cream, water, garlic, basil, and pepper; mix well and pour over broccoli. Sprinkle with buttery cracker mixture.

❖ Bake for 55 to 60 minutes or until bubbling hot and topping is crispy.

Tara Says: This casserole delivers the creamy, comforting goodness you crave after a long day. Not only is it super simple to make, but it's also a good way to get the kids to eat their veggies. Since this makes enough to feed a small army, there's a good chance you'll have leftovers. Pack some in the small bakers that are part of this set, put on their covers and take one to work the next day. You can just reheat in the microwave for an easy and tasty lunch!

Deli-Inspired Chicken Reuben Dinner

Serves 4

4 boneless, skinless chicken breasts

½ teaspoon salt

¼ teaspoon black pepper

1 (14-½-ounce) can sauerkraut, drained

4 deli corned beef slices

8 (1-ounce) slices Swiss cheese

½ cup Thousand Island dressing

1 cup soft rye bread crumbs (see Tara Says)

2 tablespoons butter, melted

❧ Preheat oven to 350 degrees F. Coat a Squoval™ Deep Dish Lid-It with cooking spray. Sprinkle chicken with salt and pepper; place on Lid-It.

❧ Top chicken evenly with sauerkraut, corned beef, and Swiss cheese. Drizzle with dressing. (Don't be skimpy with the dressing—that's my favorite part!)

❧ In a small bowl, combine bread crumbs and butter; sprinkle over dressing.

❧ Bake for 30 minutes or until chicken is no longer pink in center and cheese is all melty.

Tara Says: I have two suggestions for making your own rye bread crumbs: You can put a couple of slices of bread in your food processor with the cutting blade attachment, and pulse until you've got crumbs, or you can freeze a couple of slices and grate them with a box grater. Both are simple. I can't wait for you to try this tasty twist on one of my favorite deli sandwiches!

Sunday Night
Meat Loaf & Veggies

Serves 6 to 8

2 carrots, cut into
1-½-inch pieces

8 Brussels sprouts, trimmed,
and cut in half

8 small red potatoes,
cut in half

2 tablespoons vegetable oil

½ teaspoon garlic powder

1 teaspoon salt, divided

¾ teaspoon black pepper,
divided

1-½ pounds ground beef

¼ cup finely chopped onion

½ cup Italian bread crumbs

1 egg

½ cup water

½ cup ketchup, divided

✿ Preheat oven to 350 degrees F. Coat a Squoval™ Divided Lid-It with cooking spray. Place carrots and Brussels sprouts in a medium bowl. Place potatoes in another medium bowl.

✿ In a small bowl, combine oil, garlic powder, ½ teaspoon salt, and ¼ teaspoon pepper. Evenly divide oil mixture between vegetables and potatoes in bowls, and toss to coat. Place vegetable mixture in one outer section of Divided Lid-It. Place potatoes in the other outer section.

✿ In a large bowl, combine ground beef, onion, bread crumbs, egg, water, ¼ cup ketchup, remaining ½ teaspoon salt, and ½ teaspoon pepper; mix well. Place mixture in center section of Lid-It and form into an oval shape. (See photo.) Spoon remaining ¼ cup ketchup evenly over top.

✿ Roast for 1 to 1-¼ hours or until juices run clear. Allow to sit for 5 minutes, then slice meat loaf and serve with roasted veggies and potatoes.

Tara Says: The three-section Lid-It makes roasting three different items at one time a breeze! Plus, you can easily take this from oven to table, since it looks presentation-perfect. No more boring meat loaf nights -- I'm changing the game with this one!

Beefed-Up French Onion Soup

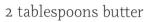

Serves 2

2 tablespoons butter

1 large onion, thinly sliced

2 cups beef broth

2 tablespoons dry red wine (optional)

¼ teaspoon black pepper

1 (¼-inch-thick) slice deli roast beef, diced

2 (1-inch-thick) slices French bread, toasted

4 slices mozzarella cheese

In a saucepan over medium heat, melt butter. Add onion and cook for 12 to 15 minutes or until golden, stirring occasionally.

Add beef broth, wine, if desired, and pepper; bring to a boil. Reduce heat to low, stir in roast beef, and simmer for 5 minutes.

Preheat oven to 450 degrees F. Pour soup into 2 (12-ounce) Squoval™ Bakers and top each with a slice of toasted bread. Place 2 slices of cheese on top of each bread slice and bake for 6 to 8 minutes or until cheese is melted.

Tara Says: Go ahead and get creative with your cheesy topping! Sometimes I mix and match two favorites, like Swiss and mozzarella, while other times I prefer a milder Muenster. No matter which cheese you choose, this soup will deliver all the richness and cozy comfort you can handle. There's a reason why this is a restaurant favorite!

Melt-in-Your-Mouth Pot Roast

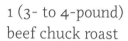

Serves 5 to 6

1 (3- to 4-pound) beef chuck roast

Salt and pepper for seasoning

4 tablespoons vegetable oil, divided

1 cup chopped onion

4 cloves garlic, minced

2 teaspoons chopped fresh thyme

2 teaspoons chopped fresh rosemary

1 cup red wine

4 cups beef broth

2 tablespoons tomato paste

3 celery stalks, cut into 2-inch pieces

3 carrots, cut into 2-inch pieces

❖ Preheat oven to 350 degrees F. Season both sides of chuck roast with salt and pepper. In a large skillet over medium-high heat, heat 2 tablespoons oil until hot. Add roast and sear on both sides. Remove to a plate.

❖ Reduce heat to medium, add remaining 2 tablespoons oil, the onion, garlic, thyme, and rosemary; cook for 5 minutes, stirring occasionally. Add wine and stir, making sure to scrape any brown bits from bottom of pan. Stir in broth and tomato paste; place beef in a 4-quart Squoval™ Baker and pour broth mixture over roast.

❖ Cover baker with aluminum foil and place in oven. Roast for 1-½ hours. Remove baker from oven; add celery and carrots. Cover and return to oven; cook for 1 more hour or until beef and vegetables are fork-tender. Slice beef across the grain. Serve with vegetables and gravy from the baker.

 Tara Says: A perfectly cooked pot roast is the equivalent to getting a hug from someone you love. They both make you feel so warm and special! The way I make my pot roast, it practically melts in your mouth. Sometimes, I cook it long enough so that I don't even have to slice it -- I just pull it apart and pour on the gravy!

"Something Special" Roasted Prime Rib

Serves 6 to 8

1 (5- to 6-pound) boneless beef prime rib

3 tablespoons all-purpose flour

2 tablespoons vegetable oil

1 tablespoon light brown sugar

1 tablespoon Dijon mustard

½ teaspoon ground allspice

1 teaspoon salt

1 teaspoon black pepper

❧ Preheat oven to 400 degrees F. Coat a 4-quart Squoval™ Baker with cooking spray. Place beef fat-side up in baker (so that the fat melts over the roast as it cooks, keeping it super juicy).

❧ In a small bowl, combine remaining ingredients; mix well. Rub mixture evenly over beef. (The mixture will be kind of thick, so you will need to sort of pat it on.)

❧ Roast beef for 20 minutes, then reduce heat to 325 degrees F. Continue cooking for 1-¼ to 1-½ hours (about 15 minutes per pound) or until a meat thermometer reaches 135 degrees for medium-rare or until desired doneness beyond that. (Even though medium rare is 145 degrees, the meat will continue to cook once you take it out of the oven.)

❧ Remove beef to a cutting board and let sit for 10 minutes before carving into slices.

Tara Says: There are lots of occasions that call for us to cook "something special." Sometimes it's because you've got company coming; other times, it's for a holiday or birthday celebration. Whatever the case, it's good to have a recipe for something special that'll make the occasion even more extraordinary. I think this prime rib really fits the bill. And if you don't have an instant-read meat thermometer, I suggest picking one up. They're not too expensive and will help ensure your meat is cooked to the perfect temperature.

Chili-Cola Braised Short Ribs

Serves 4 to 5

1 teaspoon garlic powder

1 teaspoon salt

1 teaspoon black pepper

4 to 5 pounds short ribs

3 tablespoons vegetable oil

1 (12-ounce) can regular (not diet) cola

1 (12-ounce) bottle chili sauce

2 tablespoons Worcestershire sauce

2 tablespoons hot sauce (see Tara Says)

❋ Preheat oven to 350 degrees F. In a small bowl, combine garlic powder, salt, and black pepper. Rub mixture all over short ribs.

❋ In a large skillet over medium-high heat, heat oil until hot; sear ribs on all sides. Drain liquid and place ribs in a 4-quart Squoval™ Baker.

❋ Meanwhile, in a large bowl, combine remaining ingredients. Pour chili-cola mixture over seared ribs, and cover with aluminum foil.

❋ Braise for 1-½ to 2 hours or until ribs are cooked through and fork-tender, turning and basting ribs occasionally.

Tara Says: The sauce on these short ribs is good enough to lick off your fingers! It's sweet and tangy, with just the right amount of kick. (You can reduce the amount of hot sauce in them if it's too much kick for your family.) If anyone asks what the secret to your sauce is, just say what I say, "The secret is always love." (Then, after a laugh, you can share the recipe!)

Simply Saucy Baby Back Ribs

Serves 4 to 6

1 tablespoon onion powder

1 tablespoon paprika

1 teaspoon ground cumin

1 teaspoon celery salt

½ teaspoon black pepper

1 tablespoon brown sugar

4 to 4-½ pounds pork baby back ribs, each rack cut into thirds

1 cup barbecue sauce (see Tara Says)

❧ Preheat oven to 350 degrees F. In a small bowl, combine onion powder, paprika, cumin, celery salt, pepper, and brown sugar; rub seasoning mixture over ribs.

❧ Place each rack of ribs on a large piece of aluminum foil. Wrap ribs loosely, leaving room for steam to circulate; seal edges tightly. Place foil packets in a 4-quart Squoval™ Baker.

❧ Roast for 2 hours or until meat is fork-tender. Open packets carefully, as steam will be hot. Remove from foil, slather with barbecue sauce, place ribs back in baker and return to oven for 15 to 20 minutes, uncovered, or until sauce begins to caramelize. (See photo on page 48.)

Tara Says: From my travels all over the country, I've learned that it's just not fair to tell people what kind of barbecue sauce they should use. Every region has its favorite. So, when you make these, be sure to use what your family loves best. And make sure you set out a big ol' stack of napkins, because things are bound to get deliciously messy.

Stuffed & Glazed Pork Loin Roast

Serves 7 to 8

1 (6-ounce) package stuffing mix for pork

¼ cup dried cranberries

2-½ pounds boneless pork loin

Salt and black pepper for seasoning

Cranberry Glaze

1 (14-ounce) can whole berry cranberry sauce

¼ cup orange marmalade

1 tablespoon chopped fresh parsley

 Preheat oven to 350 degrees F. Coat a Squoval™ Deep Dish Lid-It with cooking spray.

Prepare stuffing mix according to package directions. Stir in cranberries and set aside.

Cut 7 vertical slits, evenly, ¾ of the way through pork. (Be careful not to cut all the way through!) Season inside and out with salt and pepper. Evenly spoon stuffing in all slits. (It's okay if you have some leftover stuffing—you can serve it on the side!)

To make Cranberry Glaze, in a medium bowl, combine cranberry sauce, orange marmalade, and parsley; mix well. Pour glaze evenly over pork.

Roast for 50 to 55 minutes or until pork is no longer pink in center and stuffing is heated through.

 Tara Says: Cranberries and stuffing will always make me think of Thanksgiving, and this is one of those dinners you can make when you're craving those flavors. It looks like something you fussed over all day, but it's actually very easy! Once it's cooked, each person should get a slice of pork and a generous amount of stuffing. If you're making this for company, you can spoon the glaze over the pork and not the stuffing, to give it a prettier look. (See photo.)

Italian Stuffed Bell Peppers

Makes 6 peppers

1 (24-ounce) jar spaghetti sauce, divided

1 pound ground beef

1 cup uncooked instant rice

1-½ cups (6-ounces) shredded mozzarella cheese, divided

¼ cup water

1 tablespoon grated Parmesan cheese

1 teaspoon garlic powder

½ teaspoon salt

¼ teaspoon black pepper

6 large bell peppers, tops removed, and seeded

❀ Preheat oven to 400 degrees F. Spread 1 cup spaghetti sauce on bottom of a 4-quart Squoval™ Baker.

❀ In a large bowl, combine ground beef, uncooked rice, 1 cup mozzarella cheese, 1 cup spaghetti sauce, the water, Parmesan cheese, garlic powder, salt, and pepper; mix well.

❀ Stuff each bell pepper with an equal amount of meat mixture and place in baker. Pour remaining spaghetti sauce evenly over stuffed peppers.

❀ Cover with aluminum foil and cook for 40 to 45 minutes or until no pink remains in meat and rice is tender. Remove from oven, uncover, and sprinkle with remaining ½ cup mozzarella cheese.

❀ Bake for 5 more minutes or until cheese is melted. Spoon sauce over peppers and serve.

Tara Says: Mmmm...I love how each pepper is a perfectly-sized meal for one, with everything you need to leave you feeling full and satisfied. When I make my stuffed peppers, I use a rainbow of colors -- green, yellow, red, and orange--this way everyone can get their favorite. Plus, each color has a slightly different taste, with red being the sweetest!

Tuna Melt Pasta Bake

Serves 5 to 6

1 (16-ounce) package corkscrew pasta

2 tablespoons butter

2 tablespoons all-purpose flour

½ teaspoon onion powder

1 teaspoon salt

¼ teaspoon black pepper

3 cups milk

2 cups shredded Swiss cheese, divided

3 (6-ounce) cans tuna, drained, and flaked

3 plum tomatoes, cut into ¼-inch-thick slices

❁ Preheat oven to 400 degrees F. Coat a 4-quart Squoval™ Baker with cooking spray.

❁ In a soup pot of boiling salted water, cook pasta 6 to 7 minutes or until al dente (that means tender, but not mushy). Drain well and return to pot; set aside.

❁ Meanwhile, in a medium saucepan over low heat, melt butter. Stir in flour, onion powder, salt, and pepper, and cook for 1 minute, stirring constantly. Gradually stir in milk; increase heat to medium-high and cook until mixture thickens, stirring occasionally. Remove saucepan from heat and add 1-½ cups cheese, stirring until melted.

❁ Add cheese sauce and tuna to pasta in pot; stir until evenly mixed. Spoon mixture into baker. Arrange tomato slices on top, overlapping if necessary. Sprinkle with remaining cheese.

❁ Cover baker with aluminum foil and bake for 20 minutes. Remove foil and bake for 10 to 15 more minutes or until hot and bubbly.

Tara Says: You see a lot of tuna casseroles made with shells, rigatoni, or elbow macaroni, which all work great, but I like to make mine with corkscrew pasta (also known as cavatappi) because it's perfectly-shaped for holding on to all of the creamy goodness. Besides, I think the corkscrews add a whimsical personality to every bite.

Not-So-Shabby Crabby Fish Fillets

Serves 4

½ pound real crabmeat, flaked

½ cup Italian panko bread crumbs

½ teaspoon onion powder

¼ teaspoon garlic powder

½ teaspoon paprika

½ stick butter, melted

4 (6-ounce) white-fleshed fish fillets

❖ Preheat oven to 350 degrees F. Coat a Squoval™ Deep Dish Lid-It with cooking spray.

❖ In a medium bowl, combine all ingredients except fish fillets; gently mix. (Be gentle, so you don't break up the chunks of crab.)

❖ Place fish fillets on the Lid-It and evenly divide crab mixture onto each fillet. Bake for 15 to 20 minutes or until fish flakes easily. Serve immediately.

Tara Says: Why serve just a plain ol' piece of fish when you can add a fancy crab crust without even breaking a sweat? This is the easiest and tastiest way to dress up your favorite white fish. And if I'm making this for company, I like to pick up a few crab claws at the fish counter to help me decorate the platter. Presentation is everything!

Baked Shrimp in Creamy Parmesan

Serves 6 to 8

1-½ pounds large raw shrimp, peeled, with tails left on

⅓ cup grated Parmesan cheese

⅓ cup mayonnaise

2 tablespoons butter, melted

2 tablespoons chopped chives

1 teaspoon Worcestershire sauce

1 teaspoon hot sauce

❖ Preheat oven to 425 degrees F. Coat a Squoval™ Deep Dish Lid-It with cooking spray. Place shrimp in rows on Lid-It. (See photo on page 49.)

❖ In a medium bowl, combine remaining ingredients; mix well. Spoon mixture evenly over shrimp.

❖ Bake for 8 to 10 minutes or until shrimp are pink and topping is golden. Serve immediately.

Tara Says: This yummy shrimp dish is ready in less than 15 minutes and is as easy as 1-2-3. Although I usually serve this for dinner, with a few of everyone's favorite side dishes, it makes a great appetizer too (something different from the typical shrimp cocktail). Give it a try and let me know what you think!

Yankee Doodle Mac 'n' Cheese

Serves 6 to 8

1-½ pounds small shell pasta

1 stick plus 2 tablespoons butter, divided

½ cup all-purpose flour

1 teaspoon salt

½ teaspoon black pepper

3-½ cups milk

1 (16-ounce) block sharp cheddar cheese, shredded

2 teaspoons Dijon mustard

½ pound mozzarella cheese, cut into 1-inch cubes

2 cups coarsely crushed saltine crackers

❁ Preheat oven to 375 degrees F. Coat a 4-quart Squoval™ Baker with cooking spray. In a large pot, cook pasta according to package directions; drain and set aside.

❁ In the same pot over medium heat, melt 1 stick butter. Add flour, salt, and pepper; mix well. Gradually add milk, bring to a boil, and cook until smooth and thickened, stirring constantly. Add shredded cheddar cheese and mustard; continue stirring until melted.

❁ Remove from heat; add pasta and mix until evenly coated. Stir in mozzarella. Spoon mixture into baker.

❁ In a microwave-safe bowl, melt remaining 2 tablespoons butter in microwave. Stir in crushed crackers; mix well. Sprinkle evenly over top of pasta.

❁ Bake, uncovered, for 35 to 40 minutes or until top is golden and pasta is bubbling hot.

Tara Says: I'm not sure why Yankee Doodle stuck a feather in his hat and called it macaroni, but whatever the reason, it's hard not to get that tune stuck in your head. This ooey-gooey mac 'n' cheese is amazing, whether you use macaroni or small shell pasta like I use here! To avoid your sauce getting clumpy, make sure you add the mozzarella to the pasta after you've tossed it with the cheese sauce.

Sausage 'n' Peppers Italian Rigatoni

Serves 6 to 8

1 pound hot Italian sausage, cut into 1-inch pieces

2 green bell peppers, cut into 1-inch chunks

1 onion, cut into 1-inch chunks

1 pound rigatoni pasta

2 (24-ounce) jars spaghetti sauce

Grated Parmesan cheese for sprinkling

❖ Preheat oven to 425 degrees F.

❖ Place sausage, peppers, and onion into a 4-quart Squoval™ Baker and roast for 30 to 35 minutes or until sausage is no longer pink in center.

❖ Meanwhile, cook pasta according to package directions and drain.

❖ Add hot pasta and sauce to baker; mix well. Bake for 30 to 35 minutes or until heated through. Sprinkle with grated Parmesan cheese and serve.

Tara Says: I think it's pretty well-known that I love sausage, and the spicier the better. But if that's not the case for you and your family, you can easily make this dish a little milder by simply changing out the type of sausage. No matter which type of sausage you choose, it's bound to taste amazing in this Italian-style bake. After all, sausage and peppers are a classic and delicious duo that shouldn't be ignored!

The Perfect Sides

Bacon-Wrapped Brussels Sprouts

Serves 10 to 12

1 pound Brussels sprouts, ends trimmed

1 pound thick-cut bacon

½ cup brown sugar, divided

Coarse black pepper for sprinkling

❊ Preheat oven to 425 degrees F. Cut Brussels sprouts in half lengthwise. Cut each bacon slice into thirds.

❊ Wrap bacon around each halved Brussels sprout and place seam-side down on a Squoval™ Deep Dish Lid-It. Sprinkle evenly with half the brown sugar.

❊ Roast for 15 minutes, then sprinkle with remaining brown sugar and black pepper. Continue to cook for 10 to 15 more minutes or until bacon is crisp and Brussels sprouts are tender.

Tara Says: If you're the kind of person who turns away from Brussels sprouts, this recipe might just cause you to reconsider... I mean, there's bacon AND brown sugar, so you know that's going to make these taste even better. And if you want even more flavor, you can shake on a little sriracha sauce right before serving. The combination of hot and spicy with the sweet and salty bacon is really yummy!

Steakhouse Double-Baked Potatoes

Serves 4

4 large baking potatoes

¼ cup sour cream

3 tablespoons butter

1 teaspoon onion powder

1 teaspoon salt

¼ teaspoon black pepper

1 cup shredded cheddar cheese, divided

5 strips bacon, cooked crispy and crumbled, divided

1 scallion, thinly sliced (optional)

❊ Preheat oven to 400 degrees F. Scrub potatoes, then pierce each one a few times with a fork. Place on a Squoval™ Deep Dish Lid-It.

❊ Bake for 60 to 65 minutes or until tender. Let cool slightly.

❊ Cut about ½-inch off the top of each potato and scoop out pulp, leaving a ¼-inch of pulp, so that shell holds its shape. Place pulp in a medium bowl. Add sour cream, butter, onion powder, salt, and pepper, and with an electric mixer, beat until smooth. Stir in ¾ cup cheese and half the bacon.

❊ Spoon mixture evenly into potato shells, leveling it off. Place remaining potato mixture in a pastry bag with a large star tip or in a plastic storage bag with about ¼-inch cut off one corner. Pipe mixture evenly on top of each potato. Sprinkle with remaining cheese and remaining bacon, and bake for 20 to 25 minutes or until hot and top is golden. Sprinkle with scallions, if desired, before serving.

 Tara Says: Did you know that you can make these in an air fryer as an alternative to using a traditional oven? If you want to go that route, cut down the baking time about 20 percent. You may need to experiment a bit since brands of air fryers vary in size and wattage which impacts cooking times.

Any Occasion Potato Casserole

Serves 8 to 10

1 stick butter, divided

½ cup diced onion

1 (30-ounce) package frozen shredded hash browns, thawed

2 cups sour cream

2 cups shredded sharp cheddar cheese

1 (10-½-ounce) can cream of celery soup

½ teaspoon salt

¼ teaspoon black pepper

1-½ cups coarsely crushed butter-flavored crackers

✽ Preheat oven to 375 degrees F. Coat a 4-quart Squoval™ Baker with cooking spray.

✽ In a small skillet over medium heat, melt ½ stick butter. Add onion and sauté for 4 to 5 minutes or until tender.

✽ In a large bowl, combine hash browns, sour cream, cheddar cheese, soup, salt, pepper, and cooked onion; mix well. Spoon mixture into baker.

✽ In a small, microwave-safe bowl, melt remaining butter in microwave; stir in crushed crackers. Sprinkle cracker mixture over potatoes.

✽ Cover baker with aluminum foil and bake for 40 minutes. Remove foil and continue baking 10 to 15 more minutes or until golden brown and heated through.

Tara Says: When I first came across this recipe, it was shared with me as the perfect thing to bring to a funeral. I know that sounds pretty morbid, but the reason I was told this was because it feeds a bunch of people and it's full of comfort. Fortunately, I didn't wait around for a funeral to make this dish. As it turns out, comforting flavors are a big hit no matter what the occasion! So make this for your get-togethers, your graduations, and your holiday parties -- it's a winner.

Right-Sized Spinach Soufflés

Serves 2

¾ cup heavy cream

1 egg

2 tablespoons grated Parmesan cheese

1 tablespoon all-purpose flour

½ teaspoon onion powder

1 teaspoon baking powder

¼ teaspoon ground nutmeg

⅛ teaspoon black pepper

1 (12-ounce) package frozen chopped spinach, thawed and squeezed dry

¼ cup chopped water chestnuts

❊ Preheat oven to 375 degrees F. Coat 2 (12-ounce) Squoval™ Bakers with cooking spray.

❊ In a bowl, whisk all ingredients except spinach and water chestnuts, until smooth. Add spinach and water chestnuts; mix well, then pour into bakers.

❊ Bake for 20 to 25 minutes or until a knife inserted in center comes out clean.

Tara Says: Don't bother scooping out the soufflés from their bakers! These can go from oven to table with no problem. In fact, it's an easy way to add a little more presentation to your meal. Serve these with a simple chicken or beef entrée and another colorful veggie (like carrots!) for a dinner that's sure to impress your dinner date.

Balsamic-Honey Sweet Potato Wedges

Serves 4 to 5

3 to 4 sweet potatoes
(about 1-½ pounds)

2 tablespoons vegetable oil

¼ cup honey

2 tablespoons
balsamic vinegar

1 tablespoon butter, melted

Sea salt for sprinkling

 Preheat oven to 425 degrees F. Peel potatoes and cut each in half lengthwise. Cut each half into wedges. In a large bowl, combine potatoes and oil; toss to coat completely. Place potatoes in a single layer in a Squoval™ Deep Dish Lid-It.

 Bake for 25 minutes, then gently turn potatoes over and continue baking for 15 to 20 more minutes or until tender and crispy.

 Meanwhile, in a small bowl, combine honey, vinegar, and butter; mix well. Drizzle mixture over sweet potato wedges, sprinkle with salt, and serve immediately

 Tara Says: I don't always have the time to make my own sweet potato wedges. (You guys keep me busy!) So when time is limited, I use a shortcut -- a bag of frozen sweet potato fries. After they're baked, I drizzle on the delicious homemade glaze. It's an easy way to cut the prep time and still get to enjoy something I love.

Taste-of-Fall Acorn Squash

Serves 4

2 acorn squash,
cut in half lengthwise

1 cup maple syrup

¼ cup jalapeño pepper jelly

1 tablespoon butter, melted

½ teaspoon
ground cinnamon

❀ Preheat oven to 400 degrees F. In a 4-quart Squoval™ Baker, place squash cut-side up.

❀ In a medium bowl, combine syrup, jelly, butter, and cinnamon. Fill cut-side of squash evenly with syrup mixture. (See photo on page 74.)

❀ Roast for 1 to 1-¼ hours or until squash is fork-tender, brushing the cut edge occasionally with the syrup mixture. (See photo on page 74.)

Tara Says: I've got some of your favorite fall flavors right here! There's in-season acorn squash, comforting maple syrup, and heartwarming cinnamon. This side dish is going to make your house smell wonderful! Since acorn squash can vary in size, the four halves may not fit inside your baker. If that's the case, just go ahead and use the Deep Dish Lid-It too.

Roasted Mexican Corn

Serves 5 to 8

10 ears of fresh corn, husked

1 stick butter, melted

2 teaspoons chili powder

3 tablespoons chopped fresh cilantro

¼ cup grated cotija cheese

Juice of 1 lime

✣ Fill a soup pot about half full with water and bring to a boil over high heat. Add corn and return to a boil. Remove pot from heat and let stand for 5 minutes or until corn is tender; drain.

✣ Meanwhile, in a small bowl, combine butter, chili powder, and cilantro. Brush butter mixture evenly over corn and place in a 4-quart Squoval™ Baker. Roast for 18 to 20 minutes or until kernels begin to look roasted. Sprinkle corn with cheese and drizzle with lime. Serve immediately.

Tara Says: I love love love Mexican food, so I'm constantly on the lookout for new and yummy Mexican-style dishes to try. This corn (also called "elote") has popped up quite a few times in my foodie experiences, so I knew I had to add it to my repertoire of Mexican recipes. From the kickin' chili butter to the crumbly and salty cheese, this corn is phenomenal. Serve it at your next backyard get-together or for your family's Tex-Mex night!

Veggie & Cheddar Salad Toss

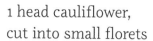

Serves 12 to 14

1 head cauliflower,
cut into small florets

1 head broccoli,
cut into small florets

1 pint cherry tomatoes,
cut in half

½ red onion, cut into ½-inch
chunks

1 (16-ounce) can pitted black
olives, drained

1 (8-ounce) block sharp
cheddar cheese, cut into
¼-inch chunks

1 cup Italian dressing

❀ In a 4-quart Squoval™ Baker, combine cauliflower, broccoli, tomatoes, onion, olives, and cheese.

❀ Pour dressing over vegetables and cheese, and toss until evenly coated. Refrigerate until ready to serve. (See photo on page 75.)

 Tara Says: This is a really simple and quick salad to throw together, but the combination of all the veggies with the cheese is just perfect. Sometimes I make it even more special by using a homemade vinaigrette or just changing up the dressing. (Caesar is good and so is a red wine vinaigrette.) Experiment and have fun with this one! And if you've got any vegetarian friends -- make sure this salad is on the menu!

Brown Sugar & Bacon Bubbling Baked Beans

Serves 10 to 12

8 slices bacon

1 onion, chopped

2 cloves garlic, minced

2 (28-ounce) cans baked beans

2 (15-ounce) cans pinto beans, drained

¾ cup ketchup

¾ cup brown sugar

❧ Preheat oven to 350 degrees F. In a large skillet over high heat, cook bacon until crisp; remove to a paper towel-lined plate to cool, then crumble. Add onion and garlic to pan drippings, and sauté until golden.

❧ In a 4-quart Squoval™ Baker, combine remaining ingredients. Add bacon and onion mixture; combine well.

❧ Bake for 1-¼ to 1-½ hours or until mixture is bubbly and slightly thickened. (See photo on page 75.)

 Tara Says: I'm a bacon lover, which means I don't just love eating bacon, but cooking with it too. In this recipe, the bacon fat adds a nice smokiness to the beans. However, if you're trying to watch your fat intake, drain off some of the bacon drippings after sautéing the onions and garlic. You'll still get some of the bacon flavor without the guilt.

Roasted Onions with Rosemary Cream Sauce

Serves 8

4 onions, peeled, ends trimmed, and cut in half horizontally

1-½ cups chicken or vegetable broth

3 tablespoons olive oil

2 teaspoons chopped fresh rosemary

¾ teaspoon salt

¼ teaspoon black pepper

½ cup heavy cream

2 tablespoons all-purpose flour

⅛ teaspoon ground nutmeg

❖ Preheat oven to 425 degrees F.

❖ Place onions cut-side up in a Squoval™ Deep Dish Lid-it. Pour broth over onions and drizzle with olive oil. Sprinkle with rosemary, salt, and pepper.

❖ Roast, uncovered, for 55 minutes, basting often.

❖ In a small bowl, combine heavy cream and flour; mix until smooth. Pour mixture over onions and sprinkle with nutmeg.

❖ Roast for an additional 20 to 25 minutes or until pan juices are thickened and onion tops are golden.

Tara Says: The first time I served onions this way, my friends thought I was nuts. They said things like, "Onions are supposed to be in a side dish, not the side dish itself!" But then they had a bite...and another...and well, the rest is history. These onions are absolutely amazing. Plus, they look and taste pretty fancy, so you can serve them for special company or for an everyday family meal.

"Souper" Creamy Rice Casserole

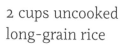

Serves 8 to 10

2 cups uncooked long-grain rice

8 ounces fresh mushrooms, sliced

½ cup chopped onion

2-½ cups chicken broth

1 (10-½-ounce) can condensed cream of mushroom soup

½ stick butter, melted

½ teaspoon black pepper

1 cup French-fried onions

❧ Preheat oven to 375 degrees F. Coat a 4-quart Squoval™ Baker with cooking spray; set aside.

❧ Combine all ingredients except French-fried onions in baker; mix well.

❧ Cover with aluminum foil and bake for 45 minutes. Remove foil, sprinkle with French-fried onions and continue baking, uncovered, for 10 minutes or until rice is tender and liquid is absorbed. Serve immediately.

Tara Says: This creamy, dreamy casserole with a crispy-crunchy topping is great for big family dinners. It pairs perfectly with chicken, beef, pork...you name it! If you're not a fan of mushroom soup, you can substitute with a cream of celery or broccoli soup. Either way, you'll have lots of flavors to love!

Chilies & Cheese Studded Cornbread

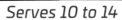

Serves 10 to 14

2 (7-½-ounce) packages corn muffin mix

1 (8-½-ounce) can cream-style corn

1 (4.5-ounce) can chopped green chilies, drained

1 cup (4 ounces) shredded cheddar cheese

2 eggs, lightly beaten

½ cup milk

½ cup sour cream

❧ Preheat oven to 400 degrees F. Coat a Squoval™ Deep Dish Lid-It with cooking spray.

❧ Combine all ingredients in a large bowl, stirring just until moistened.

❧ Pour batter into Lid-It. Bake for 18 to 20 minutes or until a toothpick inserted in center comes out clean. Let cool slightly and serve. (See photo on page 75.)

Tara Says: I don't need an excuse to find new ways to get butter into my mouth -- I just make it happen. That's why, when I serve my cornbread, I always set it out with a crock of butter. And not just any butter, but a homemade honey butter. It's really easy to do! Just add a few tablespoons of honey to a softened stick of butter in a 12-ounce Squoval Baker. Once it's well mixed, let it set for a bit, and you're done. Slather it on your piping-hot cornbread and enjoy.

Sweet Tooth Sensations

Really Chocolatey Black Forest Cake

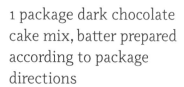

Serves 12 to 15

1 package dark chocolate cake mix, batter prepared according to package directions

1 cup semisweet chocolate chips

2 cups heavy cream, divided

1 tablespoon powdered sugar

1 (13.5-ounce) jar pitted Bing cherries, drained and cut in half

1 (16-ounce) container chocolate frosting

1 (1.55-ounce) chocolate candy bar, shaved

❋ Preheat oven to 350 degrees F. Coat a 4-quart Squoval™ Baker with cooking spray. Pour cake batter evenly into baker.

❋ Bake for 30 to 35 minutes or until a toothpick inserted in center comes out clean; let cool. Invert cake onto a cutting board and slice in half horizontally, creating 2 layers. Place bottom half back into baker.

❋ In a medium saucepan over medium heat, combine chocolate chips and ½ cup heavy cream. Stir constantly until chocolate chips melt and mixture is smooth. Remove from heat and allow to cool.

❋ In a medium bowl, beat remaining 1-½ cups heavy cream and powdered sugar until stiff peaks form. Gently fold cooled chocolate into whipped cream until well blended.

❋ Spread chocolate mixture evenly over bottom cake layer; top with cherry halves. Place remaining cake layer on top of cherries. Spread frosting on top of cake; sprinkle with shaved chocolate. Serve immediately or refrigerate until ready to serve.

 Tara Says: Do you ever really need a reason to eat cake? I don't! Actually, I like to say, "I eat cake because it's somebody's birthday somewhere!" Hey, it's true! Now, if you want to give this cake an extra-fancy look, garnish it with a combination of Bing and maraschino cherries, like I do. (See photo.)

Ricotta Strudel with Lemon Glaze

Serves 6 to 8

1 sheet of puff pastry (from a 17.3-ounce package), thawed

1-½ cups whole milk ricotta cheese

½ cup powdered sugar

½ teaspoon vanilla extract

Zest from one lemon

½ teaspoon lemon juice

1 egg, beaten

Lemon Glaze

½ cup powdered sugar

1-½ tablespoons lemon juice

❋ Preheat oven to 400 degrees F. Place puff pastry on a cutting board and unfold.

❋ In a medium bowl, combine ricotta cheese, ½ cup powdered sugar, vanilla, lemon zest, and ½ teaspoon lemon juice; mix well. Spoon mixture lengthwise down center of pastry, leaving about 3 inches on each side.

❋ Cut slits down both sides of pastry, about 1 inch apart, creating what looks like tabs. Brush each strip of dough with beaten egg and alternately crisscross strips over filling, creating a braided look. Brush top of pastry with beaten egg. Transfer to a Squoval™ Deep Dish Lid-It.

❋ Bake for 20 to 25 minutes or until the dough is puffed up and golden. Let cool.

❋ To make Lemon Glaze, in a small bowl, whisk ½ cup powdered sugar with 1-½ tablespoons lemon juice until smooth. Drizzle glaze on top of pastry. Slice and enjoy.

Tara Says: Don't feel too intimidated to make this braided strudel; it's really easy if you follow the instructions step-by-step. Trust me, when you're done, you'll feel confident enough to start creating all sorts of stuffed puff pastry braids! I like this one because it's bursting with fresh lemony goodness (inside and out!). It makes a great spring or summer treat.

Baked Personal Peach Pies

Makes 2 pies

1 refrigerated pie crust
(from a 14.1-ounce package),
cut in half

3 cups frozen sliced peaches,
thawed

1 tablespoon sugar

1 tablespoon peach jelly

❀ Preheat oven to 425 degrees F. Place both halves of pie crust on a Squoval™ Deep Dish Lid-It.

❀ In a large bowl, combine peaches and sugar; toss to coat. Arrange peach mixture in center of each piece of dough, leaving a 1-inch border. Fold the 1-inch border of the dough over edge of filling. (This way you'll be able to see the rest of the peach filling in the center.) You'll have to sort of fold or create some pleats around the edges as you do this.

❀ Place jelly in a 12-ounce Squoval™ Baker and microwave 10 to 15 seconds or until melted. Brush melted jelly over peach mixture and edges of dough.

❀ Bake for 10 minutes, then reduce oven temperature to 350 degrees. Continue baking for 20 more minutes or until lightly browned. Serve warm or at room temperature.

Tara Says: If you're still fairly new to pie-making, then this is a good recipe to start with. It's simple, there's just a handful of ingredients, and you end up with an incredible-tasting dessert. Plus, since each pie is perfectly sized for one person, you don't have to worry about having too much extra pie.

Cheesecake Swirl Pumpkin Cake

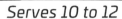

Serves 10 to 12

1 package white cake mix

1 tablespoon
pumpkin pie spice

1 (15-ounce) can
pure pumpkin

4 ounces cream cheese,
softened

1 cup powdered sugar

½ stick butter, melted

1 teaspoon vanilla extract

½ cup butterscotch chips

❋ Preheat oven to 350 degrees F. Coat a 4-quart Squoval™ Baker with cooking spray. In a large bowl with an electric mixer, beat together cake mix, pumpkin pie spice, and pure pumpkin. Pour into baker.

❋ In a medium bowl, combine cream cheese, powdered sugar, butter, and vanilla; mix well. Stir in butterscotch chips. Drop cream cheese mixture by spoonfuls over batter and swirl with a knife, creating a marbled effect.

❋ Bake for 40 to 45 minutes or until a knife inserted in center comes out clean. Let cool slightly and serve warm from oven or cool completely and serve.

Tara Says: Doesn't this look super cute in my Old World Pumpkin Patch pattern? (See photo on page 92.) I never get tired of all these fun holiday designs. And I created this one to celebrate everything that's warm and welcoming about autumn, like this cozy pumpkin cake featuring a seasonal favorite -- pumpkin spice. I can't wait to hear what you think about it!

Incredible Icebox Brookie Cake

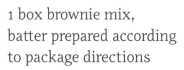

Serves 14 to 18

1 box brownie mix, batter prepared according to package directions

¾ cup milk

1 (18.2-ounce) package chocolate chip cookies, with 3 crumbled and reserved for garnish

1 (16-ounce) container frozen whipped topping, thawed and divided

❖ Preheat oven to 350 degrees F. Coat a Squoval™ Deep Dish Lid-It with cooking spray. Pour brownie batter evenly into Lid-It.

❖ Bake for 20 to 25 minutes or until a toothpick inserted in center comes out clean. Let cool, then crumble into 1-inch chunks, reserving ½ cup for garnish.

❖ Place milk in a small bowl. Dip half the cookies, one at a time, quickly into milk and place in a single layer on the bottom of a 4-quart Squoval™ Baker. Spread ¼ of whipped topping evenly over cookies. Top with a layer of brownie chunks and another layer of whipped topping. Repeat layers one more time and garnish with reserved brownie chunks and crumbled cookies.

❖ Cover and freeze for 8 hours or until firm.

Tara Says: When you can't decide between cookies, brownies, or something cold and creamy...don't -- just make this decadent icebox cake instead! It's so easy and makes the perfect summer dessert. You can start with already-baked brownies, if you're looking for a shortcut. And since it's best if this freezes for at least 8 hours, I suggest making it early in the morning or the day before you plan on serving it, so you're not rushing around.

Peanut Butter Layer Brownies

Serves 20 to 24

1 package brownie mix, batter prepared according to package directions

1 cup creamy peanut butter

1 stick butter, softened

2 tablespoons milk

1 teaspoon vanilla extract

1-½ cups powdered sugar

1-½ cups milk chocolate chips

1 tablespoon vegetable shortening

❖ Preheat oven to 350 degrees F. Coat a Squoval™ Deep Dish Lid-It with cooking spray.

❖ Pour batter into Lid-It. Bake brownies for 25 to 28 minutes or until a toothpick inserted in center comes out clean; let cool.

❖ In a large bowl with an electric mixer, beat peanut butter and butter until creamy. Add milk, vanilla, and powdered sugar; beat until thoroughly combined. Evenly spread mixture over brownies.

❖ In a small saucepan over low heat, melt chocolate chips and shortening until smooth, stirring constantly. Evenly spread over peanut butter mixture. After chocolate hardens, cut into squares.

 Tara Says: To slice the perfect brownie square, dip your knife into a glass of warm water between each cut. Then, your knife will just glide through the chocolate and peanut butter filling without getting all that yumminess stuck to it. By the way, wait till you get a taste of these; they're going to rock your world.

Bakery-Style Chocolate Cookies

Makes 1 dozen

1 cup semisweet chocolate chips, divided

1 (1-ounce) square unsweetened chocolate, chopped

1 tablespoon butter

1 egg, lightly beaten

⅓ cup sugar

2 tablespoons self-rising flour

½ teaspoon vanilla extract

½ cup chopped pecans, toasted

❀ Preheat oven to 350 degrees F. Coat a Squoval™ Deep Dish Lid-It with cooking spray.

❀ In a medium saucepan over low heat, combine ½ cup chocolate chips, the unsweetened chocolate, and butter, stirring until melted. Remove from heat. With a spoon, stir in egg, sugar, flour, and vanilla until combined. Stir in remaining ½ cup chocolate chips and the pecans.

❀ Drop half the batter by heaping teaspoonfuls, 2 inches apart, onto the Lid-It. Bake for 10 minutes or until edges are just set. Remove to a wire rack to cool completely. Let Lid-It cool slightly before repeating with remaining cookie dough. (If you have 2 Lid-Its, you can bake these all at once.)

Tara Says: Even though milk isn't one of the ingredients you need to make this recipe, you might want to have some on hand for dipping and dunking. It doesn't matter whether you do one of the nut milks or regular cow's milk, whatever you like best will be the perfect thing to wash down a plate of cookies!

Two-Minute Molten Chocolate Surprise

Serves 2 (or 1 chocoholic)

3 tablespoons butter, melted

4 tablespoons water

½ teaspoon vanilla extract

⅛ teaspoon salt

3 tablespoons unsweetened cocoa powder

½ cup sugar

¼ cup all-purpose flour

❖ Coat a 12-ounce Squoval™ Baker with cooking spray.

❖ In a medium bowl, combine butter, water, vanilla, and salt; whisk well. Add cocoa powder, sugar, and flour, whisking well after each addition. Pour mixture into baker.

❖ Microwave for 1-½ to 2 minutes or until top is set, yet center is slightly molten. (You don't want to overcook these or you'll lose all the wonderful goodness of the ooey-gooey center.) Carefully turn over onto a plate and enjoy.

Tara Says: The small baker is the perfect size to make this in. On some nights I'll share this with my hubby, Ed, but on days when I've had a really hard day, I take this to the couch, put on a good TV show, and polish it off all by myself (topped with a dollop of whipped cream). On those days, Ed knows it's best to keep his hands off my chocolate.

Donut Shop Bread Pudding

Serves 10 to 12

20 large cake donuts

1 cup raspberry seedless jam, divided

5 eggs

½ cup granulated sugar

2-½ cups whole milk

½ stick butter, melted

1-½ teaspoons vanilla extract

Powdered sugar for sprinkling

❁ Preheat oven to 350 degrees F. Spray a 4-quart Squoval™ Baker with cooking spray.

❁ Cut donuts into 1-inch pieces. Layer half of the donuts in baker. Using a spoon, dollop ½ cup jam over donuts. Layer remaining half of donuts over jam.

❁ In a medium bowl, whisk eggs and granulated sugar. Stir in milk, butter, and vanilla. Pour egg mixture over donuts; let soak for about 5 minutes. Push donut pieces down into egg mixture to coat. Dollop remaining ½ cup jam over donuts.

❁ Bake for 55 to 60 minutes or until set in center and browned. Let stand for 10 minutes, then sprinkle with powdered sugar and serve.

 Tara Says: I love going into donut shops and seeing all the different varieties they have for sale. From the jelly-filled ones to the glazed and powdered varieties, they're all so darn good! For this bread pudding, I like to use the cake donuts because they soak up the egg mixture really well. By the way, here's a tip: donuts that are about to expire (because of the date on the box) are discounted all the time. Pick up a box and make this recipe. (You don't need ones that are bakery-fresh!)

Santa-Berry Christmas Trifle

Serves 12 to 15

1 package white cake mix, batter prepared according to package directions

2 ounces cream cheese, softened

1 cup powdered sugar

1 (16-ounce) container frozen whipped topping, thawed and divided

3 cups sliced fresh strawberries plus 12 whole strawberries for garnish

1 tube black piping gel

2 (4-serving-size) packages instant vanilla pudding and pie filling mix

3 cups milk

❄ Preheat oven to 350 degrees F. Coat a 4-quart Squoval™ Baker with cooking spray. Pour cake batter evenly into baker.

❄ Bake for 25 to 30 minutes or until a toothpick inserted in center comes out clean; let cool.

❄ Meanwhile, to make Santa strawberries, in a medium bowl, combine cream cheese and powdered sugar until smooth. Fold in 1-½ cups whipped topping until combined. Cut off tip of whole strawberries and, using a plastic storage bag with a corner cut, pipe about 1 tablespoon of cream cheese mixture on top of each strawberry. Place the tip back on (so it looks like a hat) and decorate using remaining cream cheese mixture and piping gel. (See photo.) Refrigerate these until you're ready to garnish the trifle.

❄ Invert cake onto a cutting board and cut into 1-inch cubes. In a large bowl, whisk pudding mixes and milk until slightly thickened. Refrigerate for 10 minutes. Fold in 2 cups of whipped topping.

❄ Place half of the cake cubes into baker. Cover with half of the pudding mixture and half of the sliced strawberries. Repeat layers, then refrigerate until ready to serve. When ready to serve, dollop with remaining whipped topping and garnish with Santa strawberries.

Country Apple & Pear Cobbler

Serves 8 to 10

½ cup granulated sugar

½ teaspoon
ground cinnamon

½ teaspoon ground nutmeg

2 cups cold water, divided

6 apples, peeled, cored,
and thinly sliced

6 pears, peeled, cored,
and thinly sliced

¾ cup dried cranberries

2 tablespoons cornstarch

2-¼ cups biscuit baking mix

¾ cup milk

Coarse sugar for sprinkling

❀ In a soup pot, combine sugar, cinnamon, nutmeg, and 1-¾ cups water; bring to a boil. Stir in apples, pears, and cranberries; return to a boil. Reduce heat and simmer, uncovered, for 10 to 15 minutes or until tender, stirring occasionally.

❀ In a 12-ounce Squoval™ Baker combine cornstarch and remaining water. Slowly pour into fruit mixture and cook for 2 minutes or until thickened, stirring constantly.

❀ Preheat oven to 400 degrees F. Coat a 4-quart Squoval Baker with cooking spray. Transfer fruit mixture to baker.

❀ In a medium bowl, combine biscuit mix and milk just until blended. Drop by the spoonful onto fruit mixture. (Don't cover the entire top with the dough—you want the fruit to peek through!) Sprinkle batter with coarse sugar.

❀ Bake for 20 to 25 minutes or until biscuit topping is cooked through and golden. (See photo on page 93.)

Tara Says: Cozy cobblers always remind me of country kitchens with Mom or Grandma bustling over a stove, adding sugar and spices to their favorite fruits. (Don't you feel all cozy now?) When you make this, don't feel like you need to follow all the rules. If you want more apples than pears, go ahead and do it. If you could do without the cranberries, then leave them out. Let's make this your perfect version of a cozy fruit cobbler.

Tropical Treat Ambrosia

Serves 12 to 16

1 (8-serving-size) package orange-flavored gelatin

1 (12-ounce) container frozen whipped topping, thawed

2 cups sour cream

4 cups mini marshmallows

1 (20-ounce) can crushed pineapple, drained

1 (15-ounce) can mandarin oranges, drained

¾ cup chopped walnuts

½ cup maraschino cherries, drained, and cut in half

❖ In a 4-quart Squoval™ Baker, combine gelatin (right from the box, not prepared), whipped topping, and sour cream; mix well.

❖ Gently stir in remaining ingredients, cover and refrigerate for 1 hour or until ready to serve. (See photo on page 93.)

Tara Says: In my family, ambrosia is kind of a tradition. Over the years, we've come up with a few different ways of making it and, for the most part, they've all been winners. This one is light and refreshing with lots of citrusy flavors and a yummy creamy texture. Bring it to your next get-together in your baker and let everyone serve themselves, family-style.

Triple Play Chocolate Fudge

Serves a bunch of people

3 cups semisweet chocolate chips

1 (14-ounce) can sweetened condensed milk

¼ cup heavy cream

2 teaspoons vanilla extract

½ cup potato sticks, plus extra for topping

½ cup mini marshmallows, plus extra for topping

¼ cup chopped walnuts

¼ cup mini peanut butter cups, cut in half

In a medium saucepan, combine chocolate chips, sweetened condensed milk, and heavy cream. Heat over low heat, stirring constantly until chips are melted. Stir in vanilla.

Remove from heat and immediately place ⅓ of mixture into a medium bowl. Add ½ cup potato sticks; mix well. Spoon this mixture into one section of a Squoval™ Divided Lid-It. Top with extra potato sticks.

Place another ⅓ of mixture into a second medium bowl. Add ½ cup marshmallows and walnuts; mix well. Spoon this mixture into another section of Lid-It. Top with extra marshmallows.

Spread remaining ⅓ of mixture into last section of Lid-It. Top with peanut butter cups. (Do not stir these in or they will melt.)

Cover and let chill in refrigerator until firm. Cut into bite-sized pieces and enjoy.

Tara Says: This fudge is a holiday must-have and your Lid-It is a great way to showcase all the fudgy goodness! Set it out when your guests come over, so they can choose their own pieces. You can also make a few trays of this and gift the fudge along with the Divided Lid-It! I'm sure that'll put a huge smile on the faces of your friends and family.

Cinna-Apple Pull-Apart Bread

Serves 8 to 10

1 round loaf hearty white or sourdough bread, unsliced

1 stick butter, melted

½ cup brown sugar plus 2 tablespoons, divided

1 teaspoon ground cinnamon

1 tart apple, peeled, cored and finely diced

⅓ cup rolled oats

1 tablespoon all-purpose flour

1 tablespoon butter, softened

❖ Preheat oven to 350 degrees F. Coat a Squoval™ Deep Dish Lid-It with cooking spray.

❖ Using a serrated knife, create a crisscross pattern in the bread, with slices 1-inch apart and about 2-inches deep. (If you cut too deep the bread will fall apart.) Place bread on Lid-It. Evenly drizzle melted butter into all of the cuts.

❖ In a medium bowl, combine ½ cup brown sugar and the cinnamon; mix well. Add apple and toss until evenly coated. Evenly spoon apple mixture into all of the cuts. (You can use your fingers to slightly pack it in.)

❖ In a small bowl, combine remaining 2 tablespoons brown sugar, the rolled oats, flour, and 1 tablespoon softened butter; mix until crumbly. Sprinkle mixture over apples and bread.

❖ Bake for 25 to 30 minutes or until apple filling is steaming hot and bread is crispy.

Tara Says: Serve this right on the Lid-It and let everyone tear off chunks of this delicious apple bread. Not only is this dessert a great conversation starter (it's not the kind of thing you see every day!), but it's got massive crowd appeal. And with the flavors of apples and cinnamon, it's a perfect fall treat.

Upside-Down Apple Cake

Serves 12 to 15

¾ cup firmly packed brown sugar

½ stick butter, melted

2 tart apples, peeled, cored, and cut into ¼-inch slices

6 maraschino cherries, cut in half

1 package spice cake mix

1 cup apple cider or juice

❧ Preheat oven to 350 degrees F. Coat a 4-quart Squoval™ Baker with cooking spray.

❧ Sprinkle brown sugar evenly in bottom of baker and drizzle with butter. Arrange apple slices and cherry halves in brown sugar mixture; set aside.

❧ Prepare cake mix, substituting apple cider or juice for water that's called for in package directions. Pour batter into pan over apples.

❧ Bake for 40 to 45 minutes or until a toothpick inserted in center comes out clean. Remove from oven and let stand for 5 minutes. Carefully invert onto a Squoval Deep Dish Lid-It. Serve warm or at room temperature.

Tara Says: This is the warm and cozy version of an upside-down pineapple cake. The easiest way to get perfect apple slices is to peel first, then use an apple corer to remove the center. If you don't have an apple corer, almost every place that carries kitchen gadgets has them. They only cost a few dollars, don't take up a lot of space, and will be a kitchen tool you use over and over again.

Minty-Fresh Fiesta Fruit Salad

Serves 14 to 16

1-½ cups red seedless grapes

1-½ cups green seedless grapes

2 cups honeydew chunks

2 cups cantaloupe chunks

2 cups watermelon chunks

2 cups pineapple chunks

3 cups quartered strawberries

1 cup blueberries

1 cup blackberries

½ cup fresh mint leaves

¼ cup rum

1 tablespoon lime juice

1 cup sugar

½ cup warm water

❖ In a 4-quart Squoval™ Baker, combine all fruit; set aside.

❖ In a blender, combine mint, rum, lime juice, sugar, and water; blend until smooth.

❖ Pour mixture over fruit and toss until evenly coated. Serve immediately or refrigerate until ready to serve.

Tara Says: This isn't your ordinary fruit salad. This one can start a whole fiesta with how good it is! Seriously, it's one of the tastiest and most refreshing ways to serve all of your favorite fruits. And the more it sits, the better it is. I also love serving it out of the baker, since it has the ability to keep hot foods hot and cold foods cold.

Salted Caramel Munch Mix

Serves 10 to 12

3 cups oyster crackers

1 cup almonds

1 stick butter

½ cup light brown sugar

Coarse sea salt
for sprinkling

❉ Preheat oven to 400 degrees F. Coat a Squoval™ Deep Dish Lid-It with cooking spray.

❉ In a large bowl, combine crackers and almonds; set aside.

❉ In a medium saucepan over medium heat, melt butter. Add brown sugar. Bring mixture to a boil and cook for 2 to 4 minutes or until mixture is foamy and golden. Carefully pour over cracker mixture and stir until evenly coated.

❉ Spread onto Lid-It and sprinkle with sea salt. Bake for 5 minutes. Let cool completely, then break up large chunks that have stuck together and serve or store in an airtight container. (See photo on page 93.)

 Tara Says: I always like to have a few snacks that I make in advance and are ready to serve. This mix is good for anyone with a sweet tooth and has massive crowd appeal. If you want to try a different twist, you can add cashews or a pinch of ground red pepper to give it a kick. It's so good, it's hard to resist munching on it before it's time to set it out!

Index